LOOKING BACK

D1555807

PHOTOGRAPHS OF CAMBERWELL
AND PECKHAM 1860 – 1918

COVER:
Liptons, Rye Lane, 1890
BACK COVER:
Poster from Crown Theatre 1908 (original colours, red and blue)

ISBN 0 906464 10 2 PECKHAM PUBLISHING PROJECT
The Book place 13 Peckham High Street London SE15
Printed by the Carisbrooke Press (T.U.) 167a Eardley Road, SW16

INTRODUCTION

Over the last few years there has been an increase of interest in the immediate past, the years when our parents and grandparents were young. This looking back to the Victorian and Edwardian era is usually nostalgic.

These were the times when that invention of the 19th Century, the camera, was making an impact. There were numerous photographers working in South London taking pictures of weddings and other social occasions and also photographic scenes for postcards, which are well represented in this collection. Don't forget that these were still the days of the ½d post'.

From the occasions on which the camera was used (and the prints which have survived) we cannot claim to have a total picture of what life was like in those years, only a glimpse. It is evident, however, that there were still two societies in those days existing side by side. Contract the affluence of the Camberwell Council Staff Banquet (page no. 28) with the scarcely hidden abject poverty of the workmen of the gasworks (page no. 35). Contrast too the children of the Crawford Street School (page no.17) with those in the back street scene (page no.16).

The times portrayed in these photographs were periods of great change. London was booming — Camberwell becoming a thriving suburb whose population was expanding rapidly. Transport in this age saw the car and horse 'bus make way for the motor truck, motor 'bus and electric trams which ran throughout South London.

These were the optimistic years before Europe was plunged into the chaos of the Great War to be followed by the Great Depression.

"Looking Back" is a unique collection of photographs showing the optimism of these pre-war years, as well as the social contracts. It provides a unique opportunity for people to look at the life of the area in those days.

When we look back, it is usually through the eye of affection, discounting the general deprivation which afflicted many in these "Good Old Days". But — see for yourself in the photographs that follow.

Dave Pearson, Peckham Publishing Project, and
Mary Boast, Local History Librarian,
London Borough of Southwark

Most of the photographs are from the collection in the Southwark Local Studies Library at the John Harvard Library, Borough High Street, London S.E.1. telephone: 403 3507.

Many have been donated by local people; if you have similar or more recent photographs which you are willing to give, or allow to be copies, for the collection, please contact the Local Studies Library.

SECTION ONE — STREET SCENES

Denmark Hill 1899 showing the Golden Lion public house (the gap after the Golden Lion is where the Orental Palace of Varieties was demolished to make way for the Camberwell palace of Varieties, which opened in December 1899)

Denmark Hill 1897. Four shops later pulled down to make way for Orpheus Street. Note: Servants free registry office for Governesses, Cooks and Temporary help of all kinds!

Camberwell Green 1907

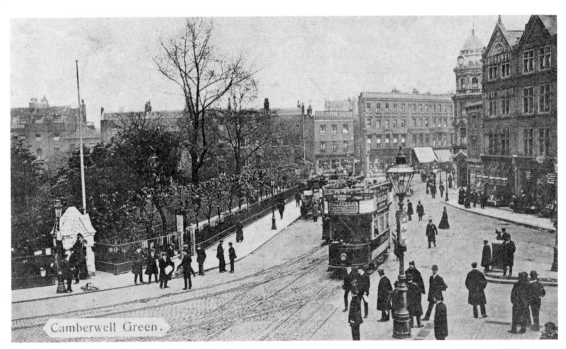

Camberwell Green 1907 showing electric trams which started in 1904 (note horse buses still in use too)

Camberwell Green 1910. Note the gent on the corner having a shoeshine!

Camberwell Church Street 1905 looking towards the Green

Camberwell road c1912 looking north

Camberwell Church Street c1905 looking east. The police station is next to Henry Turner's Hosiers shop

Camberwell Grove c1905

Grove Lane Camberwell c1900

Below. Rye Lane 1913 about 7.00pm looking south to junction of Parkstone Road
Below Right: about 10.00pm the same evening
Right: detail of photo below
Far Right: from the same vantage point looking north.
Note the **poster** advertising Houdini at the New Cross **Empire!**

11

Peckham High Street 1889 before Jones and Higgins large store was built. The Hanover Chapel is on the right

Peckham High Street 1905

Rye Lane looking north 1905

Peckham Road c1900. The South London Art Gallery is on the left, Camden Church is in the centre (bombed in the Second World War)

14

Opposite page: Top - Old Kent Road 1910
showing North Camberwell Baths (left) and Gas
works (centre)
Below - Old Kent Road 1917 showing the Lord
Nelson public house (left)

Right: Lyndhurst Road now called Lyndhurst
Way

Below: backyard of 180 Meeting House Lane

SECTION TWO — CHILDREN

A group of children in Clandon Street 1899

Crawford Street School 1906

Crawford Street School 1906
Above, dumbell exercises; below, Lyndhurst Grove School 1899

Right: A donkey ride 1907
Below: Soap box cart 1914
Below right: an attempt to take a photograph of a barrel organ and monkey but crowds got in the way!

New Church Road 1905

Bellenden School Empire Day 1907

Below: Oakley Place Mission.
The Band of Hope.

Right: detail of the
photograph below

SECTION THREE — LEISURE AND CELEBRATIONS

Camberwell Green 1908

Church procession 1909

Camberwell Town Hall, decorated to celebrate the end of the war

The Pond, Peckham Rye 1905

Opening day, One Tree Hill, Honour Oak, 7th August 1905

24

The Bandstand, Peckham Rye 1905

Trade Union banners at the opening of Peckham Rye Park 1894

War Bonds demonstration 1917. Tank parked in Vestry Road opposite Town Hall

Old Kent Road. London County Council elections 1907

Sunday on Camberwell Green 1905

Camberwell Borough Council Officers Dinner 1901

In the garden of No 18 The Terrace Peckham Road 1872

King's Dinner to celebrate the coronation of Edward VII 1902

Wedding reception in Peckham Road after wedding in St Giles' Church 1896

Denmark Hill decorated for a visit by Edward VII when he laid the foundation stone of Kings College Hospital 1909 (Joiners Arms in centre)

Street scene at election time (Bailey was the Conservative candidate!)

Workers at Gillham's Grove Park Farm Dairy 1860

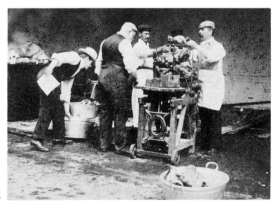

Preparing mutton for coronation celebrations 1902

Right and below:
preparing food for the
coronation 1902

Below right: Samuel Earl
wringer repairer c1905

South Metropolitan Gas Works, Old Kent Road 1902

Old Stables, Camberwell Grove c1900 (they were 300 years old then!)

Napier Lodge, Rye Lane 1860 showing a knife-board bus

Thomas Tilling horse bus outside Nunhead Railway station c1905

Oxford Circus to Peckham bus outside Jones and Higgins c1905

Postmen of Peckham Sorting Office, Hanover Street 1895

Costamonger Mr Betts chopping firewood c1900

Peckham Police Station, 1900, junction of High Street and Meeting house Lane

Dust shoot for loading barges
Old Kent Road bridge c1915

Surrey Canal near St. George's
Church c1915

Camberwell Police Station corner of
Camberwell Road and Cambewell New
Road 1890. You can see a policeman
in the doorway

LYNDHURST ROAD IN WAR TIME.

R.F.A. August 1915

Above: Army horses in Lyndhurst Road 1915   Below: YMCA hut on Camberwell Green 1917

Ye Olde Bun House c1895 96 Peckham High Street

Golden Fleece Wool Stores 1890 The Triangle Denmark Hill. Closing down sale due to demolition to make way for Metropole Theatre

Old Kent Road 1905, corner of Wagner Street

Meeting house Lane 1913

24 Peckham Rye c1900 Barrett the fishmonger (live eels are only 1s 2d a pound!)

Camberwell Church Street c1900 Geo. Waller Gents outfitters

Walworth Road
c1890

Peckham Grove c1900

No 180 Meeting House Lane 1910. There is a plaque on the wall stating that this was the meeting house which gave the street its name. This was used by the Hanover Chapel and not the Quakers as usually assumed.

Note the avertisement for the Labour Leader ''Labour's fight at the polls - some memorable victories. Ex-premiers seat won for Labour''

Camberwell Green Baths c1905. There has been little change here in 73 years

St. Saviour's Church, Copleston Road 1900

St. Giles' Camberwell Church Street 1905

Manor House Chambers 1910 Camberwell Road, 5d, 6d and 9d a night

Two views of "The Victoria" public house Choumert Road 1905.
Note the Thomas Tilling bus disappearing left in top photograph

Denmark Hill and Palace of Varieties

Camberwell Palace of Varieties, Denmark Hill 1900

Camberwell Empire c 1900 (opened 1894 as the Metropole)

838 PECKHAM. — *Wesleyan Church.* — LL.

Queen's Road Methodist Church 1905

Town Hall, Peckham Road

Peckham Road 1915 showing Public Assistance Office and Town Hall

Peckham High Street showing Police Station 1905

Peckham High Street 1905 looking in other direction showing Crown Theatre

Gordon Road Workhouse
Right: the grilles which the inmates passed the
broken rocks through. Hardly surprising that this
place was nick-named "The Bastille"

Entrance Hall and exterior of Camberwell Central Library Peckham Road 1900 (It was opposite the present Town Hall)

South London Art Gallery 1900. A fine example of Victorian opulence and confised architecture

Mary Datchelor School 1905 Camberwell Grove

Peckham High Street 1905 showing "The Crown" and the Post Office

Peckham Publishing Project would like to thank the Libraries
Department of the London Borough of Southwark for their
assistance in the publishing of this book.
We would also like to thank the following donors of the photographs
The London Borough of Southwark,
The Greater London Council, Mrs. Ruler, Mrs. Vile, Mr. O.Porter,
Mr. S. Marks.

The Peckham Publishing Project is a non-profit making body based
at The Book place in Peckham. We aim to publish work by and for
local people. If this collection of photographs inspires anyone to
write of memories of the past — bring your stories to the Peckham
Publishing Project.